This book makes total sense to me. I like that the author uses logical language to convey some very serious points. Peppered with Bible passages and famous inspirational quotes, this nonfiction offering gives helpful insight for locating one's purpose and establishing a healthy outlook. We control our own destiny and must learn to challenge ourselves and construct a solid plan for achieving our goals. The inclusion of scripture is not presented as a sermon, but as a foundation for God's plan. Udoh encourages the reader to recognize the purpose we each have as God's creatures and not to allow negative attitudes to enter into the equation.

-Lisa McCombs for Reader's Favorite
4 stars rating in Reader's Favorite

The book is a classic, a "must" read. It is both innovative, creative and rich with outstanding insights for everyday living. I started reading thinking it was just like the average book on purpose, but with each page came fresh wisdom that kept you digging for more. Good job. I am about to start reading it again.

-Victor Odiong

Drawing from personal experience and research, Onyinyechi brings a fresh perspective on finding success God's way.

-Mfon Nwabuoku

So....I've just finished reading this awesome book with an incongruous title 'Eating Your Onion'. That's one of the things that makes it special...this title. So many other things make it special. I've read some really great motivational books in my time but this precious spiel by a newbie author had me grab a pen and begin marking up passages. I was three chapters in, then went back over it all with my pen ...absorbed, engrossed and marking away for future reference.
As motivational books go, it says the usual stuff BUT....
Here's the BUT that makes this book a keeper for me (also one I'm happy to give away in order to share its truths with many)...
...it's presented in simple, relatable language that focuses on kicking you up off your complacent bottom with a smile, a laugh and a hug. I could literally feel the warmth pouring off its pages. It's not perfect, and it's not asking you to be perfect. It's challenging you to get out there and LIVE.

-Amazon Customer

Beautifully crafted for those who are at cross roads in life - seeking direction, purpose and focus. written in a simple style and with easy to follow steps. Eating your onion equips the reader with easy to apply road-maps to take you from where you are to where your dreams can be a reality.

-Amazon Customer

EATING YOUR ONIONS

Onyii Udoh

Eating your Onions by Onyii Udoh

ISBN 978-1-970072-53-2 (Paperback)
ISBN 978-1-970072-54-9 (Hardback)

This book is written to provide information and motivation to readers. Its purpose is not to render any type of psychological, legal, or professional advice of any kind. The content is the sole opinion and expression of the author, and not necessarily that of the publisher.

Copyright © 2019 by Onyii Udoh

All rights reserved. No part of this book may be reproduced, transmitted, or distributed in any form by any means, including, but not limited to, recording, photocopying, or taking screenshots of parts of the book, without prior written permission from the author or the publisher. Brief quotations for noncommercial purposes, such as book reviews, permitted by Fair Use of the U.S. Copyright Law, are allowed without written permissions, as long as such quotations do not cause damage to the book's commercial value. For permissions, write to the publisher, whose address is stated below.

Printed in the United States of America.

New Leaf Media, LLC
175 S. 3rd Street, Suite 200
Columbus, OH 43215
www.thenewleafmedia.com

CONTENTS

Acknowledgements ix
Introduction xi

Chapter 1: Unearthing Your Purpose 1
Chapter 2: Confronting the Seemingly Impossible;
conquering fear 12
Chapter 3: Be a game changer: change the game 23
Chapter 4: Flying Free: Free to Dream 35
Chapter 5: Finding A Pathway 43
Chapter 6: Eating Your Onion 51
Chapter 7: Drinking Deeply 59
Chapter 8: Living Your Life Out Loud 68

Conclusion 77
References 81

To my greatest cheerleader—my mother, the late Mrs Beatrice Onukwube Ubani (nee) Imoh. I am living it out loud. May your memory live on.

ACKNOWLEDGEMENTS

Thank you, God, for trusting me with a purpose and leading me with strength to its birthing, for all your numerous blessings on my family and me, for each day you have given us and yet to give, and for all the people around me who had made and still make life more meaningful.

Richard Udoh, my husband, friend, and lover—my one true love, thank you for being you. Your light will never grow dim.

My children Ekeminiabasi and Ukemeabasi, the spices in my life.

My siblings Chinedu Onyeador, Ngozi J. Emeka-ogbu, Victor Ubani, Nkechi Ubani—God's perfect plan and purpose can never be frustrated in our lives.

Kelsey Saldana and New Leaf Media team, thanks a bunch.

Pastor Ose Imiemonhon, my spiritual father and Pastor, May the lord replenish you bountifully.

My friends, who I met for a reason, thank you for your friendship.

Management and staff of shield academy and partners, central bank south-south entrepreneurship development center Calabar, thanks for affording me the platform to express myself.

Your life has
Purpose.
Your story is
Important.
Your dreams
Count.
Your voice
Matters.
You are born to
*Make an **impact**.*
– Anonymous

INTRODUCTION

Have you always wondered why you get fed up with your life every now and then? Why you so desperately want a change but cannot explain the change you want? Why you hate what you do despite the fact that you produce results in it? Why you always want more with every thrill of success, and above all, why you feel you are not expressing you? Do you feel your wheel spinning but lacks direction?

To make an impact in this world and achieve success on your own terms, you will need a deeper self-awareness and understanding of what is most important. Discover and accept yourself and your uniqueness; quit trying to succeed on someone else's term to prove to them; there is nothing to prove. I have been there. The answers of who you are, what to do, or how to do it might not be there at the beginning, but they will come with your genuine intent to learn and openness to change.

It was tempting to have named this book 'The Peeled Onion' as this captures the process of discovering your life purpose and walking in it. When peeling an onion, you take it layer by layer, and surely, it will sting your eyes. Such is life. Discovering your life's purpose and walking in it is one step at a time, and it comes with challenges, oppositions, and self-doubts (you name it) that seeks only to pull you down and keep you down with its pain.

However, I had chosen to name this book 'Eating Your Onion' to emphasis the meaning of one's purpose in life, what to do with it after discovering it, and how to benefit from it. Like in eating an onion, you will first peel it layer by layer which will sting your eyes, then you cut it up and that stings your eyes some more, then the eating. Onions are eaten raw to get maximum benefits from them, and that surely leaves an after taste or stench as the case maybe, and some still sting your eyes while eating them.

> ***When all you have is a hammer,***
> ***Everything looks like a nail.***
> **Anonymous**

After discovering your purpose, you must commit to growth, learn, refocus, and begin to do things differently. There is no shortage of information; it is what we do with the information we have that counts. At every stage of walking your purpose, you will be challenged, opposed, and self-doubted, but these will only be after tastes when overcame. The desire to get maximum benefits from your life purpose helps in producing the after tastes, which are life's valuable lessons.

The concept in this book is from the Christian standpoint. Why is that? You may ask what life purpose has to do with Christianity. I stand to tell you that to every man created by God, there is a purpose, and such purpose can only be fulfilled in Christ. *Thus, says the Lord, your Redeemer and He who formed you from the womb, "I am the LORD, who makes all things, who stretches out the havens all alone, who spears abroad the earth by Myself. Isaiah 47:4 (NKJV)*

No matter how open minded we get until our senses fall out, it is still a proven fact that there is a higher being out there (which can only be God) in control of everything. No one had been able to explain him away.

If you are not a Christian, I will employ you to read this book with an open mind, and if you are a Christian, I will challenge you to employ and apply what you are going to read.

We all need a companion in our journeys through life to make it shorter and sometimes easier to go through, someone who is practical, yet thinks freely without limit, who does not judge or criticize your every move, a cheerleader that believes in you when you self-doubt. Allow me introduce that person and that companion to you through the pages of this book. Each page of this book is self-discovering and self-inspiring.

It guides in realizing and accepting yourself as you are, which allows you to imagine new opportunities and take inspired action.

I would not say that I have achieved yet (you sure have not heard about me until this book), but I tell you that my life has been touched by these truths. The ray of light at the end of the tunnel has turned to a beam of light, and I cannot wait but share it with you. Just know that what you are about reading are real and true; they had changed my life, and I know they will change yours.

It will help you take your idea into reality. Consider this as **God's business plan template.**

Do not leave your life to chance.
Do not wait for chance to
Happen to you: Happen to chance.
–Onyii Udoh

CHAPTER 1

Unearthing Your Purpose

I will be forty years this year by September 2015, and I will tell you I had been like most of you reading this book, making bad choices, thinking myself smart without God's help. Yes, I had seen trickles of God's blessings; I had seen rays of light at the end of the tunnel, but it has always been an endless journey to get to the end until now. Since I took hold of these truth, I realized how near the end of the tunnel is; the ray of light has turned to a beam of light. I had always wanted to write; I had always written stories, write-ups like this (though not this put together) but never got half way because I never thought I was good enough. Other peoples' books always intimidated me after reading them. I have dabbled into a lot of businesses, which I enjoyed, but without satisfaction. Something inside kept yearning for expression but with no avail until I started studying on purpose, and at that time, I kind of found myself on the education arena—facilitating part-time in an entrepreneurship development center and a full-time vice principal administration in a secondary school. These opportunities opened my eyes and helped me touch base with that hunger that had been yearning to be expressed. I quitted my full time job, and with it came a truckload of wonderful opportunities that I had never dreamt of. I still have my part- time facilitator job, which I consider a training ground. I have learnt a lot and still learning. I have gained confidence to do what I have always longed for—to write a book and to teach (not in a formal classroom), and there, I realized I could do so in one act: write a book! There is nothing as liberating as coming to terms with your purpose. It brings with it so much joy, satisfaction, and inner peace.

What am saying is that it is never too late to start. God is a redeemer of time. *So I will restore to you the years that the swarming locust has eaten, the crawling locust, the consuming locust, and the chewing locusts, my great army which I sent among you. You shall eat in plenty and be satisfied and praise the name of the lord your God, who has dealt wondrously with you: and my people shall never be put to shame. Joel 2:25-26 (NKJV)*

Take hold of the truth above, let it become alive in you, and you have nothing stopping you in fulfilling your life purpose.

Our life purpose is that longing in our hearts as humans. The longing of being known for something, to be on top, and to excel. Nobody likes ordinariness despite the fact we more or less find ourselves on that level and remain there. The problem is that we lack the right knowledge. It is the quest for fulfillment of purpose that we have people fighting for the acceptance of their life style choices by the society. You need to ask: What you are fighting for, is it for what purpose, does it put food on your table, or does it mark you as remarkable, remembered, referred, and emulated?

The longing of our hearts wishing to be expressed, seeking to burst forth, are only thoughts, which are merely the beginning. Their fulfillment lies in our hands.

> ***I know I am good for something***
> ***I just haven't found out yet!***
> **Anonymous**

Purpose means 'an object to be reached; target; an aim; a goal' (English dictionary). Our life's purpose is same with our life's destiny. It is nothing about human efforts. It is God's predetermined end for our life. What you do per time should be a training ground for your purpose. The word of God is a road map for our destinies. Operating with a sense of destiny tampers how you act. Purpose requires discernment—ability to see what is not readily obvious. It is important to note how you see yourself and what you say to yourself when you are alone. Our biggest enemies are ourselves. Abraham and Sarah laughed when God told them they were going to have a child at their old age. They laughed because they did not believe what God had said to them or put inside them. Their actions showed their evaluation of themselves versus what God has said to them. At this point, Sarah remembered Hagar, whom she gave to Abraham to sleep with her, to 'help' God fulfill his words to them (Genesis 16:3-4 NKJV). Has Hagar not always been there? Why then did Sarah remember her, and why did Abraham accept? An African proverb says, *If there is no enemy within, the enemy outside can do us no harm.* Self-doubt is the greatest enemy within us all as humans. What we do about it, is the root of all our actions.

He who calls you is faithful, who also will do it.(1 Thessalonians 5:24 NKJV)

Sarah sought to 'help' God because of self-doubt and probably because of what has been said to her (barren woman), which she had come to believe. Nevertheless, that did not stop the promises of God. *So shall my word be that goes forth from my mouth. It shall not return to Me void. But it shall accomplish what I please, and it shall prosper in the thing for which I sent it.(Isaiah 55:11 NKJV)*

Not Abraham's wealth, intelligence, power, race, or nationality qualified him to be the ancestor of the whole nations of people. It was his faith and willingness to obey God—no matter what. What is that innate desire in your heart that brings smiles and light to your face when you think of it or engage in it? What is that you looked at or thought of at some point in your life that you decided that you could not do or talked out yourself from? Who is that person who had told you it is not possible? What is that you feel that it is too late to get started on? Those very things seeking to burst forth are your gift, talent, purpose, and **GREATNESS**. *For the gifts and calling of God are irrevocable.(Romans 11:29 NKJV)*

Most people take their greatness, talent, gift, and purpose to the graveyard with them. The wealthiest place on earth is the graveyard. In there are inventions that we will never be exposed to, ideas and dreams that never will become reality, hopes and aspirations that never will be acted upon. The question is what are you going to do about your purpose, how will you fill your time on earth, what drives you? There will never be a perfect time in your life—a right time to do a great thing. If you are waiting for that perfect moment, it is not going to happen! You have to create that perfect time, the perfect opportunity, and the perfect situation. The path to greatness is a lonely one; as such, you need to stay motivated despite all odds. Opportunity is in the eyes of the beholder; therefore, if you are not convincing enough the external force of concern will crush your dreams and vision.

And David was greatly distressed, for the people spoke of stoning him because the soul of all the people was grieved; every man for his sons and for his daughters, but David encouraged himself in the LORD his God.(1 Samuel 30:6 KJV)

No one is more capable of achieving your dream than you no matter how big the dream is. You would not have a dream God has not equipped you to bring to fruition. You only need to believe in yourself and that you can do it.

> **If you can dream it, you can do it.**
> **–Walt Disney**

Dreaming and believing in your dream produces the 'I can do spirit'. Do not be a dream chaser, put belief in your dreams, and it will only be a matter of time and it becomes a reality. The letter 'O' stands for opportunity; it is absent in yesterday, available once in today, and thrice in tomorrow. This makes it clear that plenty opportunities are ahead of you only if you can reach out to it and **HAPPEN TO CHANCE**. Your dreams will always have their chance to come alive in your life; do not let them slip away. Every Christian is blessed, but it takes the wisdom and knowledge of God to happen to chance.

I returned and saw under the sun that the race is not to the swift, nor the battle to the strong, nor bread to the wise, nor yet riches to men of understanding, nor favour to men of skill, but time and chance happened to them all. (Ecclesiastes 9:11 NKJV)

Now, make a list of those desires, talents, and gifts you have. Understand that I am not asking for only the things you already know how to do. List the things that bring joy to your heart when you think of them. The things that are struggling to burst forth. They may be things you do not know how to go about them; you may have to seek knowledge and training for them. It is never too late to learn. Do not base your list on just feelings. Base them on these points: **SMART**

S – Scalable = It should fit existing system but expand as necessary.

M – Meaningful = It should purposefully add value and solve problems as well as have profit potentials.

A – Actionable = Deployed in the real world now.

R – Relational =It should speak to your inner spirit and able to create new connections.

T – Transformational = It should change status quo, disrupt stale processes, and drive your passion.

Your dream or purpose will ultimately translate to what it brings to the table—food, fame, money and fulfillment. Creatively think on these ideas. Think outside the box. What are you going to do differently? If it is a very new idea, make it worthwhile and out of this world.

Having then gifts differing according to the grace that is given to you, let us use them… (Romans 12:6 NKJV)

There are things that you think you never need to know or that you only need to know one time in your life time but which could save your life because you had that knowledge. Unless you attempt to do something beyond that, which you have already mastered, you will never grow.

There is every need to acquire all knowledge as you can. The question should be when the messenger of misery visits you, what are you going to do, what will keep you in the game? **Your Passion and belief of whose you are!**

Oh, did I say it is going to be all easy, smooth journeys? No, I never said so, and I will never say so. Take hold of the fact that with God all things are possible. *(Mathew 19:26)* Remember He said that He knows the thoughts that He thinks towards us, thoughts of peace and not evil, to give us a future and a hope *(Jeremiah 29:11)*. Ultimately, He said, He is able to do exceedingly abundantly above all that we ask or think, according to the power that works in us *(Ephesians 3:20)*.

So what are you waiting for? What is keeping you down? Are you still considering what people will say or what they have said? People will always throw stones in your path, whether you are walking, locked up in a house, cellar, or attic. It all depends on what you make with the stones: a wall to seal yourself in or a bridge to climb over them. Remember the London bridge rhyme; the stone bridge was the strongest. You are the architect of your life. It is not important to hold all the good cards in life, but importantly, it is how well you play with the cards you hold.

Dear, grab that idea, desire that purpose of yours, and plug in!

EXERCISE

Try to identify the various needs of your society in line with your passion (purpose, talents, and gifts).

List out businesses/ventures you can venture into that offer solutions to these needs as well as having profit potential.

Carry out screening using various factors to determine the viability of the business/venture.

SCREENING CRITERIA

Ratings: 1=Poor, 2=Fair, 3=Satisfactory, 4=very Satisfactory, 5=Excellent

S/N	Ideas	1	2	3	4	5
	Factors					
1.	Availability of market					
2.	Availability of Raw Material					
3	Availability of Technology					
4	Availability of Skills					
5	Government Priority					
6	Strategic Fit					
7	Ease of Implementation					
8	Risk Exposure					
9	Profitability					
10	Cost/Benefit					
TOTAL =						

After the process of idea generation, many ideas are not relevant for the process. And working with all the idea increases the effort required for the information search and processing.

So, a process is required where the idea are screened or filtered, and only those ideas and thoughts, which are relevant and suitable for the profitable development of the process, are allowed to pass. Idea Screening is a crucial stage. The stage seeks to ensure that substantial goals and marketing objectives are set at the earlier stages of planning. Idea Screening is the process of comparing and contrasting new related ideas in order to select the most promising ones. At some point, it is important to reduce the number of ideas. Not all ideas are relevant for you. To be able to screen the good from the not so good, all ideas need to be evaluated according to some criteria, like strategic fit, technical difficulties, and market opportunities. Limited available resources make it difficult to develop several ventures at the same time, and a successful idea screening process contributes to a more focused development process with a higher possibility of success.

Idea screening helps you reduce the amount of ideas into a manageable amount, which can be developed further into models. The goal is to reduce the number of ideas without screening away 'would-be diamonds'. Please keep in mind the two potential risks in screening:

Dropping ideas too early means missed opportunities.

Developing the 'wrong' ideas means wasted resources, in terms of time and financial investment, and may put the activities in your current portfolio at risk.

In micro screening, these questions influence the scoring of each factor.

Marketing factors:

>   Potential market size
>   Compatibility of market image with your product lines
>   Relationship to competing products
>   Compatibility with existing or specified market channels
>   Access to suitable physical distribution systems
>   Fits into an acceptable pricing structure
>   Relationship to promotional methods and resources
>   Marketing resources needed to produce success
>   (Questions 1, 2, and 3)

Production factors:

>   Compatibility with existing product lines
>   Availability of processing equipment
>   Availability of raw materials and ingredients
>   Availability of technical skills to produce the product
>   Availability of production time
>   Agreement with any legal requirements
>   Cost and availability of new resources required
>   (Questions 4, 5, and 6)

Development factors:

>Knowledge needed for development
>Available knowledge and skills
>Available time and human resources
>Development funds needed and available
>Compatibility with existing strengths
>Development difficulties and risks of failure
>>(Questions 7 and 8)

Financial factors:

>Compatibility of development costs with financial resource
>Capital investment resources needed and available
>Finance needed and available for market launch and ongoing product support
>Profits or returns on investment required
>>(Questions 9 and 10)

To become a person you have never been before you must be ready to do what you have never done before.
— **Anonymous**

CHAPTER 2

CONFRONTING THE SEEMINGLY IMPOSSIBLE; CONQUERING FEAR

I believe you have arrived at a conclusion of which of your dreams reigns supreme. Bear in mind that the dream with the highest total score is not necessarily the winning dream. Your core dream might have scored low due to cost of implementation and other factors. Do not lose heart; it only means that the easiest to implement which might not be the most resounding is only a means to an end.

> *Making a decision is the death of many options.*
> **–Anonymous**

The big thumb up behind any life purpose is to dream big but start small. Everything has a small beginning. Look around you nothing came to be without growth. Some even have to metamorphose like the butterfly. So do not worry if you have to start at the larva stage. Just keep the big picture alive, and you will turn out as beautiful as the butterfly. *Though your beginning was small, yet your latter end would greatly increase.(Job 8: 7 AMP)*

Very often, we render the awesome abilities on our inside useless by giving up a situation as impossible. The five daughters of Zelophehad (Num. 27:1-11) had asked for the impossible—a possession among the brothers of their father. It has never been heard of, it has never been done, and it was seemingly impossible but not impossible. You see, they realized they had nothing to lose; all there is to be lost have already been taking by their father's brothers. They were left with nothing except their faith and boldness in God. Because of that singular act, God caused their father's inheritance to be passed to them and that became an established law that a man without a son can pass his inheritance to his daughter or daughters as the case may be.

To confront the seemingly impossible, the promises of God must become your number one focus. For every pressure or challenge we face in life, there is a promise of God in the bible that settles it. In the face of every seemingly impossible situation, there will be great oppositions. But the choice is all yours, what will hold your focus, the challenge or the project at hand? Are you going to employ the 'I cannot do it' attitude or the 'I can do' attitude? Your focus and attitude in life is very critical because whatever gets your focus plus the attitude given to it determines your experience.

> *I'd rather attempt to do something great and fail than to attempt nothing and succeed.*
> *–Robert H. Scheller*

So what if you fail? Well, at least you tried something amazing, and you have a story to tell. Nothing from nothing gives NOTHING, so it is better to try your hands at greatness. Those that attempt nothing wind up with nothing to show for it and no story of even an attempt to tell. Make sure you could always say at least I gave it a go, and with the right amount of perseverance, time, and chance, you might actually achieve something great for the record.

The major challenge we encounter in seemingly impossible situation is fear; fear of the unknown, fear of failure, and fear of what people will say, fear of losing our comfort zone, fear of rejection, etc.

To be able to move past your fears there are some life changing strategies, we will need to imbibe and deploy.

1. **Identify your fears.** Fear is on a larger part the uncertainty we feel about outcomes, circumstances, and unpredictability of future events. Fear is a mind thing that affects our emotions and which when

unchecked sends us on the wrong path of thinking and understanding of situations. As the popular definition goes,

F - False
E - Evidence
A - Appearing
R - Real

Fear has no basis in reality; they are mostly made-up interpretations about situations real only within the corridors of our minds. It only seeks to rob us of our energies, dreams, opportunities, and expressions of God's plan for our life, which is our purpose. *For God did not give us a spirit of cowardice, of craven and cringing and fawning fear, but He has given us a spirit of power and of love and of clam and well-balanced mind and discipline and self-control.(2 Timothy 1:7 AMP)*

Fear obscures the reality and exalts the challenges. When we yield to fear opportunities are passed up, we breed insecurity, which is a forerunner to depression. Insecurity chiefly gives way to bad habits like: laziness, self-doubt, drinking problem, procrastination, etc. These bad habits lead to lack of motivation, lack of development and growth, indecisiveness, etc.

To overcome fear, there is every need to identify and call out your peculiar kind of fear when facing the seemingly impossible. We face these 'impossible' situations from time to time, and they throw thought bumps at us like; there is no way, this will not work, I cannot do it, I am not going to make it, I am not qualified, etc. What are your fear thought bumps, and how do you answer to them? Do you coward under them and remain quiet or do you speak to them?

We must understand that fears are perfect opportunity for growth. You literally expand and grow in moments of fear. They are platforms of promotions. You need to make up your mind to grow over it and not under; remember fear only exist in your mind.

To overcome fear and grow, you need to be a person with a lot of initiatives. Initiatives are taking the lead or knowing what to do per time before you are told to do it. You will never apply initiative if you continuously walk in fear, and lack of initiative compromises your promotion. Wise initiative is a product of continuous thinking on the scriptures and when applied fear can be stopped at its track. Fears always bring with it a long history of things that you have attempted to overcome and failed. They are as mountains meant to be conquered. When challenging your fears, apart from having good initiative, you need to have a clear picture of your desired outcome in your imagination. The lack of these leads to complaining about your situation, which is a recipe for failure by default. Always remember that how you started does not determine how it will go with you or how it will end. Without a clear picture of the desired outcome in your imagination, you will perceive situations wrongly. When your perception of a situation is wrong, deception and manipulation comes easily, and as they take place, you lose out. Fear is a good breeding ground for deceptions and manipulations, and these seek to justify the wrong and perpetuate weakness.

The presence of God is our sufficiency or confidence. God's presence must be increased in our consciousness for the voice of fear to die. Our boldness in the face of fear increases with every voice of fear we silence with the presence of God. Whatever will not challenge you will keep you in one position. Therefore, progress is measured by the challenges you face. To take up challenges is to be confident about who you are in Christ.

2. **Grow in confidence.** Our fears are only as powerful as the depth of our confidence and the size of our hearts. A confident person is someone who takes action despite the fear that is burning within his or her heart. They are heroes and role models that build a lifetime of unforgettable experiences minus the regrets. Your greatest source of confidence is how you see yourself. Anxiety will always question your confidence. What comes to mind often plays a key role on your confidence level. The bridge between what you do and what you believe is confidence.

Despite all the opposing thoughts that might be thriving within our hearts, confidence can lead us to unbelievable possibilities and unexpected learning that strengthen our determination and move us into action. Your confidence is the key that will open many doors of opportunity, while moving you through seemingly impossible situations. A confident person transforms perception about oneself, others, and circumstances in ways that will further their cause and help them overcome their fears.

To soar to new heights, your perception about your abilities, skills, potentials, and strengths will need change. You need to perceive others differently as helpers and perceive your seemingly impossible situations as milestones in other to identify the opportunity within.

> *The more we do, the more we can do.*
> **–William Hazlitt**

Your confidence grows with accomplishments. Taking action and getting things done make it possible to do even more. You become more effective and efficient with doing more, and that grows confidence to do even more. Confident people inspire confidence in others, their audience, their peers, their bosses, their customers, and their friends. And gaining the confidence of others is one of the key ways in which a self-confident person finds success. Someone who speaks clearly, who holds his or her head high, who answers questions assuredly, and who readily admits when he or she does not know something persuades people.

> *Once you have learned to walk with confidence, you begin to release what has built up within. Life then becomes a dance and you become the music.*
> **Anonymous**

We can grow in confidence through some simple strategies:

Set small goals and achieve them. To grow in confidence effectively, you must primarily begin with small steps. Simply do something small each day that will help you to build on your levels of knowledge, confidence, and ability in relation to the fear that you are seeking to overcome.

> **Anyone who stops learning is old, whether at twenty or eighty. Anyone who keeps learning stays young.**
> –Henry Ford

- Gain knowledge and build reference; seek out new knowledge and experiences that will help you to gather a wider perception and understanding about the fears that are currently holding you back in life. Books, blogs, and movies are great places to start. For instance, reading biographies of people who overcame your kind of fears successfully will provide you with confidence and assurance that you too can successfully move through your fears in quick succession.

- Have an active imagination. Your unconscious brain does not know the difference between imagination and reality. You can use this to your advantage by simply imagining yourself overcoming your fears successfully repeatedly within your imagination. While doing this, make sure to utilize all your sensory emotions in order to vividly make the experience feel as real as possible.

- Be assertive and avoid arrogance, stand up for what you believe, and stick to your principles. The right to change your mind as you believe is yours; never come under pressure from somebody else. Avoid feeling or acting superior to others. Celebrate your strengths and successes, but recognize your weaknesses and failures. Above all, learn to be courteous and polite, show interest in what others are doing, ask questions, and get involved. Give others credit for their work—compliment and praise sincerely.

- Turn off excuses and impairing thoughts. Within each of your thoughts lie endless possibilities that can either trigger powerful and empowering emotions or likewise stimulate irrational and depressing emotional habits that will sabotage every decision you make and action you take. In fact, your experience of fear comes first with the thought of fear. Your thoughts trigger your unfounded fears of behavior. It is also important to shut off the constant excuses that roam freely within the recesses of our minds. Excuses only breed more excuses and help fears to sprout ugly flowers and weeds that clog our brains with a greater array of irrational thoughts and objections. On the other side, learn to handle failure. Accept that mistakes happen when you are trying something new. Getting into the habit of treating mistakes as learning experiences helps you start to see them in a positive light. Remember, 'what doesn't kill you, it makes you stronger!'

Learn to laugh in the face of fear. Laughter is a great form of therapy that could very well provide you with the advantage you need to help you overcome your fears. Take classes, take up an exercise routine, read books, and simply learn to teach yourself how to relax, how to find calmness and peace within your body and mind. Learn to shut off and direct your mind and body inwards when you sense fear overwhelming you

> ***Whether you think you can or you cannot-you are right!***
> ***–Henry Ford***

Confident people have some habits and characteristics that help them successfully move into a world of unlimited opportunities and potential. Some of them are:

Taking risks. Risk taking is natural to confident people. They constantly search their environment for opportunities to enhance their success and help them to move through the obstacles that are currently confronting their reality.

They learn from mistakes. They realize that it is only through the process of continuous learning that they will be able to successfully overcome their fears in ways that will further their continual attainment and progress through life.

They continually seek new experiences. They enjoy seeking new experiences, fully knowing that it is only through these new experiences that they will be able to find the opportunities, resources, learning, and confidence to help them through their fear-ridden obstacles quickly.

They accept complete responsibility. They totally accept full responsibility for their behaviors, decisions, and actions no matter what results or outcomes they experience within their reality. With full responsibility comes the acknowledgment that excuses are the forerunners to fear and lead to the development of many obstacles along one's path. A confident person will never dwell on, never complain, or make excuses that could potentially rekindle their fears in uncontrollable ways.

Faith and trust. They cultivate faith. With faith comes belief or trust, and with belief comes a sense of confidence that helps them to move beyond the obstacles that are standing in their way.

Patience: They cultivate patience. With patience comes balanced thinking, which likewise encourages better and more proactive decisions, helping them to break through the fear ridden obstacles standing in their way.

Ambition: They are ambitious people whose dreams have no boundaries. They strive for seemingly impossible goals that keep them on their toes, moving forward each day of their lives. In so doing, the courage of moving towards one destination becomes a natural thing.

Commitment: They are either fully committed to their objectives or they direct their attention on another destination.

A confident person cultivates an unshakable belief in four key areas. First, they cultivate an unshakable belief in their own ability. They totally believe that they will achieve their goals and objectives despite their seemingly impossible fears.

Secondly, they cultivate an unshakable belief in attaining a positive outcome. Instead of focusing on their fears, they continuously focus their eyes on obtaining a positive outcome that is as clear as day within the recesses of their mind.

Thirdly, they cultivate an unshakable belief in finding hidden opportunities around every corner. They understand that their fears will throw untold obstacles in their way. However, they also realize that within every obstacle, there lies a seed of hidden opportunity that they can take advantage of to move them forward along their journey towards attaining their goals and objectives.

Finally, they cultivate an unshakable belief in a higher power that is working for their betterment at all times.

As for God, his way is perfect. The word of the Lord is proven; he is a shield to all who trust in him.(2 Samuel 22:23 NKJV)

'And we have such trust through Christ toward God.' (2 Corinthians 3:4 NKJV)

'In whom we have boldness and access with confidence through faith in him.' (Ephesians 3:12 NKJV)

'Therefore, do not cast away your confidence which has great reward' (Hebrews 10:35 NKJV)

'Now, this is the confidence that we have in him, that if we ask anything according to his will he will hear us.' (1 John 5: 14 NKJV)

*Change the game. Don't
Let the game change
You!*
–Macklemore

CHAPTER 3

BE A GAME CHANGER: CHANGE THE GAME

A game changer is a newly introduced element or factor that changes an existing situation or activity in a significant way. It is that 'ah-ah moment' where you see something others don't. The transformational magic takes you from ordinary to extraordinary. Game changers are unnerving and innovative. They are ambitious with pliable vision and progressive purpose. They see the world as a complex pattern of infinite possibilities, assembling and defining them to their advantages. They find their own space then shape it into their own vision. They do not play 'the game'; they change 'the game'. They out think people who had gone before them, leveraging on them, thinking bigger, better, and different. They create their future with new and different ideas that stand out from the crowd. They are committed to becoming the best at what they do so they can inspire others. They are in control of their destiny and play the game by their own rules. Game changers are not the average people who are satisfied with mediocrity and does not mind living below their potentials; they are all about designing their life vs. taking what is given.

> *If you don't build your dreams, someone will hire you to help build theirs.*
> **–TONY GASKIN**

Opportunities and possibilities abound for those who have a dream that are willing to work hard and are crazy enough to think and believe they can change their corner of the world. If you have a vision, a passion, or a dream within your heart, you are no different from Nelson Mandela, Bill Gates, Mark Zuckerberg, Martin Luther King Jr., Barack Obama, Aliko Dangote, or anyone else who has ever changed the game and achieved uncommon success. The difference is that they simply had a vision to change their little corner of the world, and they acted on it. We may not realize it, but we are all game changers in the making; we all hold different keys for moving our world forward. The game is different for each person. It is whatever you want to be, and you are the one who make it happen. As a game changer, you are like the small hinge that swings the big door. There is no special key of advantage, luck, extraordinary talent, or privilege that separates game changers from the rest of us but only the will to become. You can breakthrough to uncommon success and limitless life. Uncommon success is not a reserved right of the rich or famous or the intellectual. Each of us can achieve uncommon success.

> ***Be a game changer, the world has enough followers.***
> **Anonymous**

Let us look at the lives of some change makers that had gone before us, and how they brought about change. We will be looking at four lives from the bible Joash, Esther, Jesus, and Saul (Paul).

JOASH: 2 Chronicles 24:1–14

Joash became king when he was seven years old (vs1). He was a game changer from birth. I believe his training as king started right away. His bath times, the food he ate, his play mates, the respect and regards he got from people around him, and most importantly the conversations he must have had with his father all spoke same to him, 'You are a king,' and his heart was on it. He understood the 'why' and the 'what'. How many seven years olds do you know that can head a family let alone a nation? It is important whom you listen to and what you chose to set your heart on.

The bible reckoned that he did what was right in the sight of the lord (vs 2). He had a vision to repair the house of the Lord and called the uncle Jehoiada, the chief priest and all the priests and Levis, and charged them to quickly collect money from the Israelites according to the commandment of Moses, but they did not carry out his instruction (vs 5-6). In the first place, that was their normal duty, and if they have been about this duty, the house of the Lord would have been maintained needing no repairs, but no! They were lacking on the duty even when charged to do it.

> ***Life is like cameras…. focus on what's important, capture the good times, develop from the negatives, and if things don't work out, take another shot***
> **Anonymous**

Joash had to change the game and play by his own rules; he did not sit waiting for the uncle to do as he charged him. He disrupted the norm; he took charge of the given space to bring to birth his vision. He made a chest, set it outside at the gate of the house of the Lord, and declared throughout the land that they bring their monies as Moses commanded (vs 8–9). The people were inspired and did as they were charged. In everyday, there was more than enough. The chest came in overflowing (vs 11). Joash completed the work and had extra to make articles for the house of the Lord (vs 14). With Joash changing the game has nothing to do with age but hunger for change. With every game change comes liberation of destinies around (vs 12–13). The people who worked on the repairs were paid. The sellers of the materials bought for the repairs equally benefited.

> ***For every vision left to die because of set of rules, destinies die.***
> **Anonymous**

ESTHER: Esther 1-10

The book of Esther started with king Ahasuerus's feast of one hundred and eighty days and extra seven days for the inner caucus members. On the seventh day of his seven-day feast, he sent for his queen, Vashti, to be brought wearing her royal crown to show her off for she is beautiful to behold (1:1-11). To the king, this is the toping on the icing. His feast had been about showing off his riches, splendor, and excellence of his kingdom, and he had left his queen for the last show because

Vashti tops them all. Vashti refused that honor (1:12). Yes, it has never been done; it was not the norm to be showcased as an item, but this was a different game, and she did not know it. The king had never celebrated for one hundred and eighty days and seven extra days for inner caucus members. It was a change of game, but Vashti did not know. This angered the king and his wise men, and she lost her seat as queen (1:13-20).

> ***Change is the essence of life. Be willing to surrender what you are for what you could become!***
> **–Anonymous**

You see, the only way to make sense out of change is to plunge into it, move with it, and join the dance.

The king and his wise men declared a beauty pageant for the king to select a new queen. The preparation of which will take one year and in the kings palace. Her uncle Mordechai enrolled Esther. Esther was not the only maiden under Hegai, the custodian of the women, but she was the only one recorded to have found favor in his eyes, and the only one he readily gave beauty preparations besides her allowance. He also gave her seven choice maidservants to attend to her and moved her to the best place in the palace (2:8-9). Think about it, why was she favored, did Mordecai speak on her behalf or did she lobby for Hegai's attention? None of that. I believe Esther had a disposition about her different from others that marked her as a game changer, and Hegai recognized it. On the other hand, Esther acknowledged that to play this game and win, she must recognize and accept help from the one that knows the already existing set of rules (2:15). You see, there are destiny helpers attached to every destiny. Any game changer that must fulfill destiny must acknowledge and accept the help of the destiny helper. Esther won the contest and became queen. A situation arose, where Haman, the king's right hand, plotted and sent out a decree for a set date to kill all the Jews because Mordecai refused to bow down before him (3:5-12). Mordechai remembered the game changer that God had set before them, and he, being her mentor, sent to her to go to the king on their behalf. Esther counted the cost and knowing what could befall her if she goes unsummoned to the king. She called upon a higher authority—God. *The kings heart is in the hand of the Lord, like the rivers of water. he turns it wherever he wishes. (Proverbs 21:1)*

She employed the Jews and her maidservants too, to fast for three days with her seeking God's face on the major change of rules (4:11–17).

You see, every problem is a chance for you to do your best but not without an enabler. God was Esther's enabler. On the third day of the fast, she defiled the set rules and played by her rules. She sought the king's face without being summoned. Esther changed the rules and challenged authority, but she did not go demanding attention, whining for the rules to be changed. She had a plan, she used her influence, and she watered the king's appetite and kept him guessing. She got him where she wanted, and with that everything changed.

> ***When the winds of change blow, some people build walls and others build windmills.***
> **–Chinese Proverb**

Esther had a choice to cut off Mordechai and cocoon herself in the safety of the palace, but she chose to step out, took the risk, and changed the rules. No game is ever changed without risks.

JESUS CHRIST: Mathew, Mark, Luke, and John

The gospel according to the four books above is about Jesus changing the game for humanity. The Pharisees, Sadducees, and others looked for a military messiah who would deliver the Jews from Roman domination. But, Jesus came offering deliverance in form of salvation from sin (the worst kind of domination). He offered hope to the hopeless, love to the unloved, healing to the hurting, etc. He pushed the game to the next level right from his conception. He is the ultimate game changer, first and only one to be conceived by the Holy Spirit (Luke 1:26-36), brought forth by a virgin in a manger (Luke 2:4-7). His birth was noised abroad by all of heaven (Mathew 2:1-11, Luke 2:8-18). Men of worth came bearing gifts and bowing to him as king even as a baby. There were people waiting for his birth, to welcome him on earth before they could die. On meeting him in the temple as an eight-day-old baby, they knew they had met with an ultimate game changer. They knew that humanity would never remain the same (Luke 2:25-38). You may say that was circumstantial; it had nothing to do with him. He was only a baby. Let us then look at adult life.

At twelve years of age, Jesus pushed the buttons of knowledge. He was found amongst the teachers, entreating them with his teachings, questions, and answers. He left them with a knowing that they have met with a game changer (Luke 2:42-47). Everywhere he turned to he left an 'aha moment'.

He turned water into the best wine ever at a wedding (John 2:1-10), and left the guests wondering over the change of unspoken ceremonial rules—serving the best wine first instead of last as it happened.

- He proclaimed the fulfillment of scripture among the people, which is (him) God made flesh, he knew himself-his purpose on earth and declared it with boldness (Luke 4:16-30, John 8:12-59).
- He healed on Sabbath days (Luke 6:6-10, 13:10-13, 14:14).
- He healed people with leprosy (Luke 5:12-13, 17:12-9).
- Delivered people possessed with demon) Luke 4:33-36, 40-41, 6:17-18, 8:27-35, 9:38-42).
- He ate with sinners (Luke 5:29-32. 7:36-39, 15:1-2).
- He forgave sins (Luke 5:18-26, 7:48-50).
- He defended the harlot (John 8:3-11).
- He paid his tax with money gotten from a fish's mouth (Mathew 17:27).
- He was always celebrating with his disciples (Luke 5:33-35, 6:1-5).
- He taught in parables and questioned and answered the people in parables (Luke 5:36-39, 6:39-49, 7:47-49, 8:5-8, 10:30-36, 12:16-21, 13:6-9, 15:11-32, 16:1-13, 18:1-17, 19:11-27, 20:9-18).

He confounded his forerunner, John the Baptist, who felt he knew Jesus's path better because he announced his coming (Luke 7:18-27).

He set new laws (Luke 6:22-38, 11:37-41, 12:22-59, 19:45-46).

He fed thousands at a time with five loaves, two fishes, and seven loaves, few fishes. He got twelve baskets and seven large baskets full in return respectively (Luke 9:12-17, Mathew 15:34-38, 16:9-10).

He calmed the sea (Luke 8:22-25).

He walked on water (Mathew 14:25).

He had a great following (Luke 12:1).

He proclaimed the future (Luke 21:6-36).

He was betrayed with a kiss (Luke 22:48).

He never defended himself (Luke 22:53-54, 64-71, 23:2-3, 9-10).

He went to the cross willingly of his own accord and died for humanity (Luke 23:26-46, John 19:10-11, 16-18). Yes, Jesus had all it takes to have stopped his death on the cross. He is the son of God but chose to be man. He had his misgiving about His death (Mark 14:33-34, Mathew 26:37-38). However, He yielded to the ultimate authority –GOD the Father (Luke 22:41-44, Mark 14:36-41, Mathew 26:36-46).

He rose on the third day (Luke 24), just as he had raised the dead in his lifetime (Luke 7:12-15, 8:49-55).

Signs and wonders went forth as he took his last breath, strong holds were broken, and the wall between humanity and divinity shattered (Mark 15:37-39, Mathew 27; 50-54).

His miracles and signs were too numerous for recording (John 20:30, 21:25).

Jesus fulfilled the scriptures, the vision of God for humanity. His purpose on earth was complete (John 19:36-37, Mathew 3:15).

Divinity (Jesus) as man restored grace to man and reconciled man to his maker.

> *Change is hard at first, messy in the middle,*
> *And gorgeous at the end.*
> **–Robin Sharma**

He challenged every known rule; he stirred the still waters and took the perfectly laid out carpet off the feet of everyone. He knew the game, knew when to bend it, change or adapt the rules. he played by his own set of rules, to his aim: 'the salvation of humanity'. Rather than pursuing personal purity by following a given set of laws, Jesus seeks out collective well-being, justice, and righteousness more than chasing after morality. He knew who He is, knew it is enough to do the job—'change the game'. Jesus operated from this knowing, he was fearless and bold in the face of what people will say. He made sure he left enough evidence for humanity to believe in him. He made his time count using his gifts for his purpose. Conscious awareness of who you are and what your gifts (strengths) are the 'wild card' in every game change.

(SAUL) PAUL: The book of Acts

When Jesus was crucified, the High Priest thought that His death would put an end to His radical ideas. But with Jesus death, His resurrection, and the baptism of the Holy Spirit, His followers became even bolder in proclaiming that Jesus is the promised Messiah (Acts 2:3-47). Saul was a brilliant, ambitious, and faithful young Jewish man, completely committed to the Law and made it his personal challenge to completely stop the heretical followers of Jesus. To him all they do was the worst type of blasphemy. He showed up at the stoning of Stephen, and it is obvious he approves of the death sentence (7:58, 8:1-3). Saul set off to Damascus with the death warrants in his hand and ready to imprison, beat, and even murder anyone who mentions the name of Jesus (9:1-2). On his way, he suddenly meets a true immovable, unchangeable opponent, the ultimate game changer 'Himself', who changed Saul's game and placed him in the part of his true purpose on earth. He was stalled on his perceived purpose of his life, made blind in that direction.

But, by God's power, Ananias goes and lays hands on Saul and heals him, then baptizes him. He got his sight back with focus on the right purpose of his life. Saul's murderous rage against the followers of Christ transforms into the strongest passion ever witnessed in a Christian's life, and he becomes one of the greatest preachers to truth sharing with a people he once believed were on the wrong side of God's eternal story (9:1-31). To be counted as a brother in Christ after his attempts to ruin the church, must have been a great shock and astonishment for Saul. What a blessed introduction into the Christian family. There was no word of reproach for his persecuting activities. No vehement words that Saul should pay for what he has done. No silent ridicule—nothing—but the soothing sound of a brother from the lips of other individuals who has experienced God's grace.

> ***I wanna change the game in a way where i'm not knocking nobody out of the way, not claiming to be the best at this or that, but just doing wonders with the gifts i've been given.***
> **–Anthony Hamilton**

The above seems like Saul's thoughts. Was never part of the apostles that were with Jesus, he was taken into the fold after his encounter with Jesus and was taught by the apostles, changed his name to Paul set off to change his world with the gift he has been given which he believed in. Paul was the most travelled and most radical of his time. He had extreme results from his focus on change. Your belief and focus is very important in changing the game. If you focus on results, you will never change. If you focus on change, you will get results.

Characteristics of a game changer:

    They know their purpose and value.

    They have mentors they leverage on and eventually outgrow.

    They recognize and use their destiny helpers.

    They know when to act and do so with boldness.

    They know the risk involved in their game and are fearless.

    They employ all tactics to change situations and influence drive.

- They recognize that there are destinies attached to them waiting to be set free.
- They are like catalysts. They prepare people to see beyond what they think is possible.
- They help redirect the perspective of followers.
- They recognize their ultimate authority, God, and plug in.

Some of the personality traits that fuel game changes successes are:

- Good communicator
- Pit bull
- Resolve
- Open minded
- Committed
- Radical passion
- Good listener
- Courageous
- Active compassion
- Influencer
- Makes mistakes
- Uninhibited creativity
- Connects well
- Unrelenting hustle
- Prioritizes vision
- Fanatical focus
- Extreme boldness
- Flexible or adaptable
- Trusts in God

The question is not who the game changers are but rather, will you be a game changer? To survive and live, we must start the change process, like the eagle we must also pluck our unpleasant memories, negative habits, and fixed mindset. Only freed from the past burdens can we take advantage of the present. Let go of the negative old limiting beliefs, open up, and let yourself fly again like a pruned eagle.

A turkey was chatting with a bull, 'I would love to be able to get to the top of that tree like other birds', sighed the turkey, 'but I haven't got the energy.'

'Well, why don't you nibble on some of my droppings?' replied the bull, 'They are packed with nutrients.'

The turkey pecked at a lump of dung and found it actually gave him enough strength to reach the lowest branch of the tree. The next day, after eating some more dung, he reached the second branch. Finally, after a fourth night, the turkey was proudly perched at the top of the tree. A farmer promptly spotted him, and shot him out of the tree.

*Bullshit might get you to the top, but it will not keep you there.

Anonymous

CHAPTER 4

FLYING FREE: FREE TO DREAM

There are people who are working where they do not want to work. There are people who hate their jobs, but they keep on getting up to go to it. Often we lose all hope and think this is the end; remember it is just a bend not a bus terminal. Do you think it was your alarm clock that woke you up this morning? Try putting it besides a dead body, and you will realize that it is the grace of God that woke you up.

If only we can see life, the wonderfully simple way young children see life. It is a way of seeing in which anything is possible.

So why is it, then, that we forget how to dream the beautiful dreams of our childhood? Could it be that we have been taught to forget, have been told how complex life is, told we cannot do this, and we are not smart enough, fast enough, or talented enough to pursue that? And in hearing that—in responding to these words whose effect is to close doors and narrow our thinking—we make ourselves poor in our imagination and in leading a meaningful life?

> *All men dream but not equally. Those who dream by night in the dusty recesses of their minds wake in the day to find that it was vanity; but the dreamers of the day are dangerous men, for they may act out their dreams with open eyes to make it possible.*
> *– T. E. Lawrence*

Maybe we quickly discount our dreams as mere fantasies because we could not immediately imagine *how* these dreams would become reality.

The truth is, just because our minds does not immediately know how it will accomplish something, does not mean it is impossible.

It can be uncomfortable to let go of the need to know *how* as this can make us feel vulnerable or silly. But if we are to dream to our full potential, it is essential that we learn to have faith in our abilities. This means we should dream wildly without trying to know how these dreams will become reality. There will come a time when we should develop a plan, but initially we should enjoy the beauty of our dreams and trust that a path exists to realizing them.

Our dreams will need us to develop our character and capability in order to be fulfilled. Just because we have a dream, does not mean that we are mature enough to accomplish it yet. It takes growth, counsel, evaluation, and adjustment along the way. God given dreams will require us to develop our character, competence, and commitment to our dreams. Our dreams are like seeds, and every seed needs to be watered, nurtured, cared for, and worked on in order to come to fruition. They require us to begin with what we already have, but dream 'BIG' and be willing to pay the price for 'CHANGE'. There seems to be times in life when we are most receptive to change.

When we hurt so much that we are forced to change. Jesus tells about this type of individual in Luke 15. The parable of the prodigal son exemplifies that sometimes, it is only when we are looking up from the depths of the life that we truly see a need for change and make the commitment to do it. In all hurt needs to be great enough to create a yearning to change.

It is the same boiling water that softens the potatoes that hardens the egg; it is about what you are made of not the circumstances.
–Anonymous

People are inclined to change when they become bored and restless. Everyone experiences this at some point or another in life. Dissatisfaction can be healthy when it urges us to begin to dream dreams. Death is apparent for any person that becomes so satisfied in his life, his thoughts, and his deeds that he ceases to be challenged to do greater things in life.

The realization that we can change brings about change. Far too often, people fall into the trap of believing that just because things were a certain way for a long time, they will always be that way. We fail to realize that we can change. Things can change. Often, we settle into a rut and a certain way of thinking, and we accept limitations that have no room in our lives. We need to believe for change.

How many of us have ever found ourselves throwing a well-deserved pity party? How often have your thoughts turned to 'If only. . .'?

If only I had finished college.

If only you had a job or a better job.

If only you had not been cheated by a friend.

If only your husband or wife had not had that affair; you were the one who had the affair.

If only my parents had not divorced.

If only your husband, your wife, or your parents did not have a drinking problem.

If only your father, your brother, or whoever it was had not stolen away your innocence through an abusive relationship or rape.

'If only . . . if only. . .' Our pain, regret, and sorrow over past failure, unfulfilled expectations, or tragedy can paralyze or destroy our ability to dream. We find ourselves locked in a prison of misery and regret without any hope for tomorrow. We owe it to ourselves to dream and see our dream become reality. THINGS MAY GET WORSE BEFORE THEY GET BETTER. Do not expect overnight success. Likely quitting points to break through are only bus stops not a parking lot. Do not stop dreaming.

It is unrealistic to believe that growth is going to be automatic. We are unlikely to move from cruising along enjoying the status quo and suddenly move in an upward direction.

When we desire to make a change in our lives, it mostly comes with a dip in the road. Before the upswing, we experience a pothole and the bottom falls out. All too often, people quit when the unexpected dip in the road comes. Therefore, they never see the growth and improvement that they were hoping for. Once again, their dreams are broken. Expect the dip in the road. Do not quit on the downturn, be prepared, and work harder to minimize its depth and width. If you keep at it when things get tough, you will soon find the upswing and growth you are looking for. *He gives strength to the weary and increases the power of the weak. Even youths grow tired and weary, and young men stumble and fall. But those who hope in the LORD will renew their strength. They will soar on wings like eagles; they will run and not grow weary, they will walk and not be faint. (Isaiah 40:29-31 NIV)*

If there is something that you want to change in your life, do not let obstacles hold you back. Even if you do not know how, commit to finding a way. Because if you keep on waiting, you are gambling that you will have the time and the opportunity to make it all happen at some time in the future.

That is a hell of a gamble to take with your one and only life. The key is to stop pushing and striving against the world and, instead, realize that change comes from the inside out. It is time to take a closer look at the only thing you can really change—**yourself**. In order to create real and lasting change on the outside, you need to organize your internal world and dream freely. This begins with a simple question: **what do you want?**

There is no shame in not knowing immediately. In fact, I ask myself this question almost every day, and the answer seems to change constantly depending on my mood, environment, and recent experiences. However, over time, you can identify a theme, and as you peer into those similar answers, you will eventually discover a purpose.

By purpose, I mean that driving desire to change the world in a specific way. The best way to discover what you want is to continually ask yourself the 'w' questions: what, why, how, when, where, and who. They will guide you through this process and eventually bring you to your identity. After all, you were born to change the world, so stop saying, 'I can't' and have a little faith!

Increase Your Knowledge

Dreaming of improving the world needs you to develop the wisdom and skill to make your dreams come true. This begins with learning. This step requires some courage. It is going to take time and humility to submit yourself to the rigors of self-education. You will need to take a class or two, read books, browse blog posts, dig through Wikipedia, and maybe even watch a documentary or two. The good news is that once you get started, you will discover a burning passion that drives you forward. This is what you have always wanted, and even if you cannot have it today, at least your one-step closer to realizing your destiny. When I concluded that I was going to be a writer to lend my voice to many, I started reading more. I registered with a book club, I read blogs, magazines, and about anything my eyes can settle on. I read to gain information, to see how and learn how people write, and to find a writing style that speaks to me. I took note of quotes on billboards, flyers, etc. I wrote down conversations in movies and speeches with friends. When I read them in my quite moments, I cancel out some, reword some, and meditate on some. Those were my defining moments; I have that book right beside me as am writing now. I flip through comments and write ups I have had for some time and share them.

Be Open to Feedback

Feedback is essential for progress. It is nature's way of letting us know when to turn and how fast to move. You need to look at the results of your actions and ask, 'Is what I am doing working?' Track your progress.

Remember, life is a journey. It is important to choose a worthwhile destination and take those first steps, but after that, sit back, relax, and enjoy the ride. After all, it is all you have got. Make it count!

> ***Life is only traveled once: today's moment becomes tomorrow's memory. Enjoy every moment, good or bad, because the gift of life is life itself.***
> **–Anonymous**

Greatness is a lot of small things done well day after day.
—T. D. Jakes

CHAPTER 5
FINDING A PATHWAY

To do whatever your hands and your purpose determine before to be done.' (Acts 4: 28 NKJV)

A lot of us become comfortable. We stop growing, stop wanting anything. We become satisfied. There are people getting ready to go to jobs they do not like, jobs that make them sick. You see, when you are not pursuing your goal, you are literally committing spiritual suicide. Your purpose is already in-built. *'I have raised you for this very purpose, that I might show you my power and that my name might be proclaimed in all the earth.' (Exodus 9:16 NIV)* You just have to let go of what you think should be and allow what is meant to be. Finding your path is simply living life to the fullest. It comes with an obsession that willingness to take one-step at a time toward what feels most alive to us. However, be careful obsession can become dangerous, if not balanced with setting goals. When you do not have some goals out there, you are stretching for, reaching for, that takes you out of your comfort zone, you will not realize some of those talents, gifts, and abilities that you do not know you have. Stop waiting for your neighbor to make it happen for you; it may never happen. If you are waiting on your mother or your father, they may be so old-fashioned in their thinking that they may not understand the opportunity that you have, and it will never be done.

The worth of a thing is measured by how much a person is willing to pay for it.
–Pastor Ose Imiemohon

What reason can you remember that you can call on, that you can reach out to, that can make you get back up? Find that reason if you are not where you want to be or if you do not have what you want to be at this particular point in your life. It has nothing to do with the system but everything to do with the fact that you are not making the sacrifice. Make that dream a reality because if you do not, you will be working for somebody to make his or hers a reality.

> *The ignorance of the oppressed person is the strength of the oppressor.*
> *–pastor Ose imiemohon*

Therefore, my people have gone into capacity because they have no knowledge.(Isaiah 5:13 NKJV)

You have the right and potential to be everything you know you can be. Just as the birds know when to fly south, so do you know what feels most alive in you. Grab the winning idea from your screening, and follow this guide.

Write the vision down

Have a picture of what you success looks like or what it should look like. *Write the vision, and make it plain on tablets that he may run who reads it.(Habakkuk 2:2 NKJV)* Your path has nothing to do with what people have done. You are you. It is your life.

Set goals and intentions

Think about what is important to you. How will you like to be remembered in your absence? Make a list of things you feel that sound really exciting and wonderful and choose the best. They could be the things you will like to achieve in the next six months, one year, or even three years (long-term goals). To make your goals more powerful use the SMART method (Peter Drucker):

S – specific (or significant)
M – Measurable (or meaningful)
A –Attainable (or action oriented)
R – Relevant (or rewarding)
T – Time bound (traceable)

Ninety-five per cent of people procrastinate on their goals. Be different from them.

State your mission

Have a clear strategy. Visualize what it will look like when you are done and decide what you want. Define your terms, stop to think about why set the goals you have chosen and determine if it is possible. Rank your goals to help you focus on the most meaningful. Assess the level of commitment to each goal. Create sub goals to make each goal more achievable. Identify obstacles in the way of achieving your goals.

Stop the search

Stop trying to control everything.

Do not worry that your life is turning upside down. how do you know that the side you are used to is better than the one to come? – **RUMI**

Therefore, I tell you, stop being perpetually uneasy (anxious and worried) about your life, what you shall eat or what you shall drink, or about your body, what you shall put on. Is not life greater [in quality] than food and the body [far above and more excellent] than clothing?

Look at the birds of the air; they neither sow nor reap nor gather into barns, and yet your heavenly Father keeps feeding them. Are you not worth much more than they? And who of you by worrying and being anxious can add one unit of measure (cubit) to his stature or to the span of his life? [Ps. 39:5-7.] And why should you be anxious about clothes? Consider the lilies of the field and learn thoroughly how they grow; they neither toil nor spin. Yet I tell you, even Solomon in all his magnificence (excellence, dignity, and grace) was not arrayed like one of these. [I Kings 10:4-7.] But if God so clothes the grass of the field, which today is alive and green and tomorrow is tossed into the furnace, will He not much more surely clothe you, O you of little faith? Therefore, do not worry and be anxious, saying, What are we going to have to eat? Or what are we going to have to drink? Or what are we going to have to wear?

For the Gentiles (heathen) wish for and crave and diligently seek all these things, and your heavenly Father knows well that you need them all.

But seek (aim at and strive after) first of all His kingdom and His righteousness (His way of doing and being right), and then all these things taken together will be given you besides. So do not worry or be anxious about tomorrow, for tomorrow will have worries and anxieties of its own. Sufficient for each day is its own trouble. Mathew 6: 25-34 (AMP)

Believe in yourself, and use what you have:
Stop been suppressed by other peoples' opinions and ideas of the way things 'ought to be'. Continue on you newly discovered path. The more you focus on your voice and that of encouraging friends, the more you will grow in the belief of yourself. We are not meant to all go in one direction. By taking one step every day, putting aside over thinking, you will realize that all you need are deep down within. You will find the right direction, may be not the direction you anticipated, but it will work out fine. Consider the lepers in 2 Kings 7:3-4 (KJV). Accept where you are, work with what you have, and listen to what feels alive, captivating, thrilling, and intriguing.

Manage your time
We do not have forever to live here on earth. It is okay to test your abilities, dedicate your time to them, find a routine, and track your progress. Prioritize expressing yourself in whatever way you find to express your ideas and purpose. I am doing mine. To be fully yourself and find your path in life, you must create time for it. Time

is always in scarce supply; you can never have enough time to what you really have to do. However, time can be created for anything that you set as a priority to achieve because the vision is for an appointed time.

'A time to be born and a time to die, a time to plant, and a time to luck what is planted.' (Ecclesiastes 3:2 AMP)

Turn down the distractions

Things like television, gossiping, chatting, and internet surfing only serve to keep you stuck. Turn them down and allow possibilities. This would not be easy, but try getting out of you and try the right things out. Surround yourself with like-minded people and share. Discard assumptions, expectations, and outside programming.

Be patient and find motivation

Do not expect your purpose to be delivered via express mail. Honing your path in life is a continual part of your life journey. Treat yourself and the world around you with patience. Reinforce your positive actions. Shake up your routine and make out time for yourself. Shifts in perspective are easily explored and nurtured, when you give yourself the space physically and emotionally.

Trust and depend on God alone

Most of us have faced disappointments, which have taught us that we can only depend upon ourselves. But living the life God has called us to means unlearning that lesson. Instead, we are meant to rest in God's understanding.

We may know in our minds that He possesses all wisdom, but sometimes, trusting Him completely like that can be tough. Therefore, each day we must consciously lay aside our own plans and expectations—and surrender to His plans. Proverbs 3:5, 6 of NKJV says, '*Trust in the Lord with all your heart, and lean not on your own understanding; in all your ways acknowledge*

Him, and He shall direct your paths.' The more you trust God, the more He will amaze you.

Ask right questions and learn to listen

> *'Curiosity will conquer fear*
> *even more than bravery will.'*
> *–James Stephens*

Skillful questioning needs to be matched by careful listening so that you understand what people really mean with their answers. Your body language and tone of voice can also play a part in the answers you get when you ask questions. Questions are powerful ways of:

- Learning
- Relationship building
- Avoiding misunderstanding
- Defusing a heated situation
- Persuading people

When asking questions, be curious, be open-minded, engage yourself with listening, and dig deeper.

An Eagle was sitting on a tree resting, doing nothing.

A small Rabbit saw the Eagle and asked him, 'Can I also sit like you and do nothing?'

The Eagle answered, 'Sure, why not?'

So the Rabbit sat on the ground below the Eagle and rested. All of a sudden, a Fox appeared, jumped on the rabbit, and ate it.

'To be sitting doing nothing, you must be sitting very, very high up.'
–**Anonymous**

CHAPTER 6

Eating Your Onion

Onions are one of the inexpensive most versatile vegetables native to Asia and the Middle East. They are now indispensable healthy vegetables in breakfast to super of almost every cuisine. They can be served caramelized, marinated, roasted, baked, fried, and raw.

Retail sales of whole peeled or diced or sliced onions are freshly sold to consumers. Commercial food companies make food items like salsa, soups, sauces, and breaded appetizers like onion rings with pre-cut onion products.

In Egypt, onions are highly regarded. They were used as currency in the payment of workers that built the pyramids. Onions are considered an object of worship and stands as a symbol of eternity to the Egyptians. They buried their kings (Pharaohs) with onions believing they have preservative effects leading to eternal life. To them, the circle-within-a-circle structure of the onion symbolizes eternal life. The old and new kingdoms had paintings of onions on the inner walls of the pyramids and in the tombs. Onions are shown upon the altars of their gods, mentioned as a funeral offering and portrayed in various forms and sizes on the ceremonial tables of their great feasts.

There were often pictures of Egyptian priests holding onions in their hands or covering an altar with a bundle of their leaves or roots. Pelvic regions of the bodies of mummies had been found with onions on them. The thorax, ears, and the collapsed eyes of their dead were not left out. On the chest most times are found flowering onions. The sole of the feet and legs also get to have onions attached to them. Example, King Rames IV, who died in 1160 BC, was buried with onions in his eye sockets. The theory was that onions may have been believed to have the ability to prompt the dead to breathe again because of their strong scent. Some other theory believed that it has magical powers because of its strong antiseptic qualities, and this could be handy in the afterlife.

Onions has been eaten as food on its own.

We remember the fish we ate freely in Egypt and without cost, the cucumbers, melons, leeks, onions, and garlic. Numbers 11:5

The Israelites eat onions as food at a time in Egypt, and they liked it to the extent that they lamented its absence during the exodus.

In the early sixth century BC, Charaka Sanhita in India celebrated the onion as medicine, which is good for digestion problems, for the heart, for vision, for the bone or joints, and as a diuretic.

In Greek, athletes consumed pound of onions, drank the juice and rubbed them on the bodies to fortify themselves.

The Romans were regular eaters of onions. They were the ones that carried onions into the provinces of England and Germany. They believed that onions could cure vision, induce sleep, and heal toothache, dog bites, mouth sores, dysentery, and back pain. During the excavation of the doomed city, gardens where found with telltale cavities in the ground where onions had grown.

In Europe during the middle age, Europeans had made onion part of their main cuisine. Apart from serving as food for all, it was also used to alleviate headaches, hair loss, rent payment, wedding gifts, etc.

Early American pilgrims found strains of wild Onions throughout North America. The native American Indians had used it in numerous ways to treat cold, coughs, asthma, repel insects. They eat them raw or cooked, used them as seasoning in sauces, as dressings, as a component in dyeing processes, and even as toys. In 1648, they planted bulb onions as soon as they could clear the land in North America.

In China, onions have been used to treat coughs, throat infection, breathing problems, and bacterial infections.

The World Health Organization (WHO) had recognized onions as a curative in the treatment of asthma, bronchitis, cough, and common colds. They support its use for treatment of poor appetite, urinary tract disorders, and prevent atherosclerosis (cholesterol deposits in the arteries). Onions suppresses the growth of likely harmful bacteria in the colon. They can also reduce the risk of tumors developing in the colon.

With the world onions production on the increase, onions are now the second most important horticultural crop after tomatoes.

Onions not only provide flavor, they also provide important nutrients and health-promoting natural occurring chemicals. High in vitamin C, onions are a good source of dietary fiber, and folic acid. They also contain calcium, iron, and have a high quality protein. Onions are low in sodium and contain no fat.

Onions contain antioxidants compounds that help delay or slow the oxidative damage to cells and tissue of the body. Studies have indicated that flavonoid with its potent antioxidant actions helps to eliminate free radicals in the body, to inhibit low movement of fats through water inside and outside cells in the body, to protect and regenerate vitamin E (a powerful antioxidant), and to inactivate the harmful effects of chelate metal ions.

Other studies have shown that consumption of onions may be beneficial for reduced risk of certain diseases. It may prevent gastric ulcers by sifting free radicals and by preventing growth of the ulcer-forming microorganism.

Onions contain fiber and folic acid. Vitamin B helps the body make healthy new cells. It encourages a healthy heart in many ways, including lowering blood pressure and lowering heart attack risk and stroke. It also helps in digestion, inflammation, healthy immune system, and improved bone density in older women, among many others.

You may be wondering why all that about the onion, and what has onion to do with your life purpose or vision. With a clear understanding of the above description, uses and benefits of the onion, take hold of you life's purpose and follow me.

As dated as the onion is on earth, growing in the wild uncultivated, so is your life's purpose, inside of you unrecognized by none. You are born with it. It is deeply ebbed in you, sprouting up here and there, asking to be recognized and cultivated.

> ***If you hear an onion ring, answer it.***
> **—Anonymous**

Maybe nobody believes in you. People around you mock your purpose or vision, or they value the vision but regard you as incapable and that brings a lonely feeling, a feeling of timidity. What will you do? Will you let that ring of onion you are hearing die without answering it? When things do not work out for you, when things happen you did not anticipate. What are the reasons that you can think of that can keep you strong? Think of only why you are doing it. If it was easy, everybody will do it, like the peeling of the onion that hurts the eyes, but we still peel it because we want to use it in our foods and get all the benefits it has to offer. Researchers had devised many ways and method to peel the onion so it does not hurt the eyes; like freezing it for some minutes before peeling and cutting, peeling and cutting under running water and leaving the root end on. Do these methods stop the onion from hurting the eyes? No, they only reduced the effects to the eyes and lengthened the process of peeling and cutting the onion. This shows you that there is no shortcut to success. To cultivate, activate, and implement your purpose here on earth, you must pass through the process. You will never ever be successful until you turn your pain into greatness, until you allow your pain to push you from where you are to where you need to be.

> *life is like an onion. You peel it off one layer*
> *at a time, and sometimes you weep.*
> **—Carl Sandburg, American Poet**

Stop running from your pain—embrace your pain. Your pain is going to be a part of your path and your pattern that will challenge you to push yourself. An old English rhythm goes, *Onion skins very thin, mild winter coming in. Onion skins very tough, coming in winter very rough*. As our faces are different so are our purposes. Never compare yourself with anyone even if your talents or purposes are the same. The application can never be the same. That two people have good voices that sound alike does not mean they will sing the same kind of song. That am prompted to write a motivational book do not mean I have to write like everyone else. We all have to find and know our path because our challenges are all different. The tougher the challenges, the deeper, lasting, and heavier the rewards will be. Challenges breed character and tenacity. You cannot achieve your life purpose without these.

> *I will not move my army without onions!*
> **Ulysses S. Grant**

No one had ever made any meaningful impact in this world without challenges. Success and challenges go hand in hand. It is easy to be at the bottom of the ladder. It does not take effort to be a loser. It does not take any motivation or drive to stay down there on a lower level, but it counts on everything in you to get up from there. You have to have the heart to say, 'I will' . . . 'I am going to challenge myself'. The onion can sprout in the wild without cultivating, so can you succeed without your doubters or praise singers. Remember David (1 Samuel 30:6). You need to encourage yourself, trust God, follow you passion, and be committed to yourself. You cannot flavor dishes with the onion and get its benefits without crying; you cannot pursue your dreams, succeed, and enjoy its benefits without challenges. The onion contains many nutrients, it helps a lot of health issues, and leaves an after taste, so does your vision have a many sides to it, ties to many lives, benefits you, and help you on many issues and will surely leave you marked either good or bad—you choose.

> *The onion and its satin wrappings is among the most beautiful of vegetables and is the only one that represents the essence of things. It can be said to have a soul.*
> **—My Summer in a Garden by Charles Dudley Warner**

A farmer grew excellent quality corn. Every year, he won the award for the best-grown corn. One year, a newspaper reporter interviewed him and learned something interesting about how he grew it. The reporter discovered that the farmer shared his seed corn with his neighbors. 'How can you afford to share your best seed corn with your neighbors when they are entering corn in completion with yours each year?' the reporter asked. 'Why, sir?' said the farmer. 'Did you not know? The wind picks up pollen from the ripen corn and whirls it from filed to field. If my neighbors grow inferior corn, cross-pollination will steady degrade the quality of my corn. I must help my neighbor grow good corn. Call it power of collection, call it principle of success, call it the law of life, the man is focused. Bent on achieving his purpose; grow award winning excellent corns.
Anonymous

CHAPTER 7

DRINKING DEEPLY

We all have the opportunity of a lifetime, but it means nothing if we do not take advantage of it. In taking advantage of our opportunities, we will surly fall, and when we do, we should always try to fall and lay on our back. Because if we can look up we can get up since, we will likely be looking at what is passing us by or waiting for us which will surly create a desire to get up and get to it. Never have your back on your dreams. If you want something bad enough, go out and fight for it, and work day and night for it. Give your time, peace, and sleep, if all that you dream and scheme about life seems useless and worthless without it. It is time now, if you want to make this your decade you have to say yes to your life, yes to your dreams, yes to your unfolding further, yes to your potential. The difference between people who are able to make a success of their life purpose, visions, and dreams and those who do not is the ability to turn vision into action. Having many good ideas is not enough to make you successful. It is what you make of it. You need to define your path from vision to action, your need to drink deeply in what you believe. The free dictionary online defines drinking deeply as to take in eagerly through the senses or intellect, figuratively in the sense of taking in something through the mind or the senses. How eager are you to make your vision a reality? You will need to acquire all the knowledge that you can, seek for all the help that you can get, and spend all the time available in the application of the acquired knowledge.

A little learning is a dangerous thing; drink deep or taste not the pierian springs. there shallow draughts intoxicates the brain and drinking largely sobers us again.
–'An Essay on Criticism' 1709 Poem, Alexander Pope

In Greek mythology, it was believed that drinking from Pierian spring would bring you great knowledge and inspiration; thus, Pope explains how if you only learn a little it can 'intoxicate' you in such a way that makes you feel as though you know a great deal. However, when 'drinking largely or deeply', you become aware of how little you truly know.

The value of drinking deeply is to apply what you have learned. Sipping gives you variety, you get to sample many ideas, you gain a lot of awareness, but you do not devote time and energy to gain their benefits. You have your attention bouncing from one idea to the next not gaining much in the way of application.

A truly good book teaches me better than to read it. I must soon lay it down and commence living on its hint. What i began by reading, i must finish by acting.
–Henry David Thoreau

As you sip from the stream, you need to look for what is most important and most useful to you, and then you need to drink deeply on them; spend time studying it. Ask yourself, 'what part of this do I need to apply to my work? How do I begin executing on these ideas?' Information is essentially free and completely abundant especially with the internet available. You carry a good part of the collected knowledge of human kind in your hands (our smart phones). Not everything that flies by you is worth your time or your energy. Small sips are not going to quench your thirst. What is worth your time and energy deserves more of your time and energy. When you can articulate and speak about your vision in a clear way that it inspires you and inspires others, your life becomes about something bigger, something that is deeply fulfilling and feeds your soul.

At the beginning stage of activating your purpose, you will find yourself wearing many hats, usually. because you cannot afford the extra hands. It is okay, but please do not stagnate at this point realize when to let go to avoid over parenting or micro managing. It takes humility and leadership to realize that people will do things differently than you might have, but that does not make their way wrong. Humility to know that you do not know everything and leadership to build a team that does know what it needs to know. Most spend so much time working on their weaknesses and trying to be everything, but the problem is that growth will only happen to the limits of the talents of that individual. You want it to grow to the talents of entire team. It takes a group to move a vision beyond paper. If you hold on too tightly, it does not grow. You will need to learn to work on your vision not in your vision. To do so, consider these points:

Recognize and improve your talent/purpose.

> Find what stirs your heart, follow it, and commit to building it into a skill. Surround yourself with people of like talent; learn more from their routine practice, and let them coach you. Respect the complexity of your talent; the more you develop it the more elaborate it becomes. Do not trifle with it.

Have a plan.

> Outline your goals and how you will get there. Leave room for the unknown, always consider alternatives. They should not be casted on stone. Be open to re-visitation and review.

Wear the hat that fits.

> Focus your attention on the strengths and passions that support your vision. It should be what you are passionate about and excel at and that adds to the value of your vision.

Get a mentor.

> Find someone who has a process for listening and drilling down on issues. Someone that challenges you in a positive manner, shares best practices with you, and holds you accountable to your action plan items. Find someone who has a higher level of expertise in your field or other fields and who is as passionate as you are about growing and developing visions.

Know when to let go.

> Delegation is hard, but healthy and necessary if you expect to grow your vision and as a person. People do not learn by doing repetitive work. They learn by making judgment calls that are not always right. They learn by being given the authority and responsibility to do a better job.

Acknowledge the journey.

> It is so easy to get frustrated when you are trying to fix the puzzle between where you started and where you want to be. Recognize and acknowledge that the journey is a part of your creative process that makes your vision meaningful.

Expect the unexpected.

> You are going to hit roadblocks along the way—these are simply opportunities to rest, re-evaluate, tweak, and adjust your plan accordingly. Your action plan is not cast on stone. You can always change the path of your vision.

Make room for bounce backs.

> More than once, you will likely be knocked down and thrown off course. No good story goes without a little bit of conflict. Your success depends on your ability to get back up and keep going.

Prioritize time.

> Count the cost, and plan your priorities based on your personal values and passions. Make time for what matters most, things that will move you closer to achieving your vision. As Nelson Mandela said, 'There is no passion to be found playing small—in settling for a life that is less than the one you are capable of living.'

Align your mindset.

> Put yourself in a powerful state of mind to take action. It is critical not only take the actions you need to take, but also important so you will be EFFECTIVE when you do. When you BELIEVE, you can accomplish your goals and are doing so in service of your vision. Your actions will be so much more potent. When you doubt and question yourself, your actions are muddy. It is all in the mind!

I'm convinced that about half of what separates the successful entrepreneurs from the non-successful ones is pure perseverance.
—Steve Jobs

Get organized.

> Know what you have to do and where to find what you need to do your work. Being organized about your dreams and goals will help you accomplish them faster.

Be committed to your vision.

> Wanting something is not enough. You have to get yourself into a space of commitment to start taking action. Allow your vision to commute you to a path—to an action course.

Be a good communicator.

> Be clear in your communications. Transform that vision into action by talking and with clarity. 'For

assuredly, I say to you, whoever says to this mountain, "Be removed and be cast into the sea," and does not doubt in his heart, but believes that those things he says will be done, he will have whatever he says.' (Mark 11:23 NKJV) A clear vision attracts people, destiny helpers to it.

Be people orientated.

Build relationships; be genuinely interested in people that you meet and those around you

> *Life is not about waiting for the storm to pass. it is about learning how to dance in the rain.*
> **–Anonymous**

Transparency

Make a display of trust; it attracts the best people and builds loyalty.

Distinguish yourself.

Create a niche for your vision; explaining the niche you unquestionably own is a better path than trying to win every deal on every point. Differentiate yourself from the opposition rather than just try to 'kill' them.

Keep them coming back.

Do something to invest in your customers' experience after the sale. We are caught up in getting new customers that we sometimes forget how to keep them thrilled one year later.

Be courageous.

This simply means taking action in the face of fear, not necessarily that the fear has gone away. Fear can cripple even the boldest dreamer but courage triumphs.

Accountability

> Show integrity and a solid relationship with what you say you are going to do. This will take practice and patience and oftentimes, kindness. Be kind to yourself if you fail at some point. Accountability is HUGE part of getting the stuff done, and it ensures alignment.

Reinforce the good.

> Congratulate yourself and the people with you on the good aspects of your actions. We are always battling problems instead of reveling in the good stuff; the good stuff is what makes our actions fun and is kind of the whole point.

Learn to give back.

> Give your supporters something wonderful, free. Give them something for free to show you care, and they will reward you ten-fold. Give and it will be given to you: good measure, pressed down, shaken together, and running over will be put into your bosom. For with the same measure that you use, it will be measured back to you. (Luke 6:38 NKJV)

When I stand before god at the end of my life, I would hope that I would not have a single bit of talent left and I could say I used everything you gave me.
—Erma Bambeck

CHAPTER 8

LIVING YOUR LIFE OUT LOUD

Do you feel like you are 'sleep-walking' through life? Do you wish you had more freedom? Do you wish you had more adventure? Do you wish you had more time? Do you wish you had more love? Do you dread Monday mornings? Are you looking forward to what is coming up next? Are you living your best life?

> *You only have one life, so live it up, drink it down, laugh it out, face your fears, and regret nothing.*
> **—Anonymous**

Living it out loud is a big deal. It makes a big deference. You cannot accomplish big things on your own. It is an unpleasant fact. Great ideas, businesses, projects, adventures, and everything else that you can dream up that big cannot be done in isolation. To accomplish your dream and produce results you are going to have to open your mouth and share what is in your heart. Your ideas and your passion—they want to be heard by others! Everything holding you to a life, you do not want to live is a prison created by your own mind. That does not mean you can just wish yourself into a new life, but it does mean that you can actively work towards living life to the fullest.

It is a critical-changing step on the path towards making your dreams a reality. Doing so takes courage, vulnerability, and risk. You will be letting people know what you really, really want for your life that thing that you want to make happen. It may fail miserably, completely not work or people might think you are completely nuts for going for it.

But finding courage to let people into your heart and share what you are dreaming about is not always easy. That raw vulnerability to create something, share it, and put yourself out there is scary. It is also very powerful and liberating. It is the secret ingredient for making your dream go from idea to reality.

> *If you ask me what I came to do in this world,*
> *I will tell you, I came to live out loud.'*
> **–Émile Zola**

Your life experience is up to you to create. Why settle for anything less than what you can get? You deserve nothing but the best. In the past years of my life, I had found myself struggling to fit into every mold that passes by me. I was trying to live, but there was no live in any of the molds. It lights up with the excitement of a new thing but fizzles out cold before you know it. I felt out of alignment, thought there was something wrong with me. Living out your life purpose comes with a burning passion, abundant joy, dreaming with your eyes open, and you will find yourself smiling at nothing. It is freedom; it is liberating. You will be more conscious, more alive, and more importantly you will be experiencing life on a completely new level. It is an amazing experience, and I want you to experience that too. Here are a list of timeless principles I use to live my best life, and I hope they'll help you to do so too:

Live every day on a fresh new start. Do not be held back by what happened yesterday, the day before, the week before, the year before, and so on.

> *The only good reference to the past is the lesson you*
> *learnt that is relevant to solve future problems.*
> **Pastor Ose Imiemohon**

Own your personality. Be true to who you are. Stop trying to please other people or be someone else. It is better to be an original version of yourself than an exact duplicate of someone else. Trying to please everyone is a great way to ensure you never do anything remarkable.

> *Your time is limited,*
> *so do not waste it living someone else's life.*
> —**Steve Jobs**

Understand that personality traits are not static. Everything is changeable. If you're being held back by aspects of your personality, whether its laziness, social awkwardness, mediocre intelligence, know that these are all things that can be improved if you're willing to work on them, instead of accepting them as unchallengeable personality traits.

Stop complaining and be proactive. Stop complaining about your problems and work on them instead. Stop waiting for others around you to do something and take action yourself instead. Make conscious and deliberate choices. When you do not choose, circumstances choose for you, and you are never leading: you are following or catching up—or worse, living in 'default' mode.

Always think next time. Do not think about things you cannot change or unhappy things because they are limiting. Instead, focus on the things you can take action on. That is the most constructive thing you can do in any situation. Focus on WHAT you want first, before you think about HOW to do it. Anything is possible, as long as you set your mind, heart, and soul to it.

Create your own opportunities. You can wait for opportunities to drop in life. Or you can go out there and create your own opportunities. The latter is definite and much more empowering. Live more consciously each day. Stop sleepwalking through life. Your life is something to be experienced, not coasted through. Dream with your eyes open.

Do not be a crab in the bucket. You've heard the expression 'crabs in the bucket'— it's the tendency crabs have for pulling other crabs back down right when they're about to climb out. When you break from the norm, you will get pushback from your loved ones. It is not jealousy. They genuinely care for us. But people living the life society tells them to live get scared when they see others going for it. Even if they do it subconsciously and even if it is out of genuine concern, it is still harmful. It creates a culture of conformity, mediocrity, and quiet desperation. Do not be a crab in the bucket.

Overcome your fear and be committed to growth. Get out of your comfort zone. Find out you have a pulse. Let something give you butterflies in your stomach. This is how you know you are alive—how you grow into something new. Every fear overcome is a freedom gained. Do the thing you are afraid of. Cross them off the list. Make it a game. Soon, you will be invincible.

Discover new talent, create a new habit, or break an old one.

We don't know who we are until we see what we can do. But we don't find this out until we try something new.

Make it a game. How many things can you get under your control? How many bad habits can you convert? There is a great sense of empowerment when you feel you are in charge of your life. This helps you get there. Learn a new instrument, take an art class, play with a digital camera, sign up for a salsa class, take up cooking, plant a garden, pick up a needle and thread, try mountain climbing, go scuba diving, camping, or kayaking. Find something that interests you and explore it. You never know what will come out of it.

Set some life values and honor them. Every one of us has our own set of ethics, principles, and moral codes. Live true to them every day. Also, live in full alignment with your purpose. When you strip everything else away, your word is all you have. Do what you say you are going to do. By honoring your word, you honor yourself. And it doesn't feel good when you don't. So, make it a habit. Value your integrity, and keep your promises. It is a good life practice. It is a good business practice.

Set goals and take action on them. Know what you want to achieve for each stretch of your life, and make sure to look back and see if you actually made the progress you wanted. This list will constantly evolve, and you will not reach every one of your goals, but writing your goals down will make it more likely that you will achieve them.

Unclutter. Start from your computer, then your table, your room, your bag or wallet, and your home. The more you throw the unwanted and old stuff away, the more room you are creating for new things to enter. Create your inspirational haven. Turn your room into a place you love. Do the same for your work desk. Get rid of things that make you unproductive. Surround it with things that inspire you and trigger you to action

Value yourself. Give yourself permission to make mistakes, to shine, to look beautiful, to accept (instead of correct or dismiss) praise, to have bad days, to get angry, to cry, to laugh, to scream, to take the day off. Permission to take a nap, go to sleep early, to get a massage, to do nothing, and to succeed. Life is about being here now, in all your full range of emotions, mood swings, wins, and losses. Give yourself permission to live out loud today. Others may be more educated, skilled, or talented in one or another area, but there is something magnificent and valuable about what you have to offer this world that, in comparison, is equal.

> ***The purpose of life after all is to live it, to taste experience to the utmost, the reach out eagerly and without fear for newer and richer experiences.***
> **—Eleanor Roosevelt**

Do not allow yourself or anyone else to diminish it. Stop idolizing anyone else's gifts and dismissing your own. No one has to agree with you in order for your opinion to matter. Stop waiting for consensus. You matter. Your opinion matters. The nature of living out loud is that some people will agree with you and some people won't. You will never get consensus. So, stop looking for it. The only question you have to ask is, does your opinion matter to you? Claim it. Own it. And know that with new information, it could change tomorrow. Life is transitory. Live in the evolution.

Embrace gratitude, express gratitude. Be grateful for everything you have today, and everything you will get in the future. Let the people who have touched you know of your gratitude toward them. You will be surprised what a little act like this can do. If you do not tell them, they will never know.

Love generously. Treasure and love yourself. *Be kindly affectionate to one another with brotherly love, in honor giving preference to one another.' (Romans 13: 8 NKJV)* Spread random acts of kindness and senseless acts of beauty. Hatred is already rampant. We need to tip the scales the other way. Love is a far more powerful emotion and has far-reaching consequences. Living out loud means loving out loud. And ironically, the more you love, the more love you have to give. Offer your help where you can, and do your part in making the world a friendly place. We are all in this together. As Gandhi preached, be the change that you wish to see happen. You would be surprised by the impact you have. *For wherever there is jealousy (envy) and contention (rivalry and selfish ambition), there will also be confusion (unrest, disharmony, rebellion) and all sorts of evil and vile practices.(James 3:16 AMP)*

Always smile and laugh more often. Learn to have fun. Sing at the top of your lungs. Dance in the rain. Run barefoot and feel the ground underneath your feet. Release of your self-imposed shackles and be free.

Leave in the moment and relish every bit of it. A time out with your best friend, a walk by the park, the breeze on your face, quiet, alone time, watching the sunrise or sunset or a movie, soak in all these little moments of life, they are what make up your life. Activate your social life.

Take care of your body. Eat healthy when you can, get a good night's sleep, and exercise. Your only connection with this world is through this fleshy meat vehicle we call our bodies. Take good care of it. Improve your posture. Did you know that your posture and body language not only shapes how people see you, but it also shapes how you feel about yourself?

Constantly work on improving yourself. If you are not doing something to improve yourself every day, then you are not going to reach your goal. Take care of your mind. Stop feeding it a constant stream of junk. A little downtime is all right, but do not dedicate every free hour you have to watching realty TV, watching gossip blogs, checking sports scores, and doing other stuff that requires little mental energy. Even the news can rot your brain with its constant barrage of negativity and biased sensationalism.

- Surround yourself with the type of people you would want to be. There is a saying that you are the average of your five closest friends. If you constantly spend time with negative people, you will become negative as well. If you spend time around people with no ambition, you will find your own dreams slipping away as well. On the other hand, surrounding yourself with awesome people who want the same things you want in life will set you up for success. Hang out with people who you compatible with like-minded people, people who are positive, successful, strong achievers, and positive for your growth. You are after all the average of the five people you spend the most time with.

- Get yourself out there. This applies for everything. Get out there geographically. Go out, travel, and explore the world. Set sail into the sea. Go backpacking by yourself, and visit as many countries as possible. Get on a road trip, and visit the different places that come out. Get out there. Stop sticking to routines and comfort zones. *You did not choose me, but I chose you and appointed you that you should go and bear fruit, and that your fruit should remain, that whatever you ask the father in my name he may give you. (John 15:16 NKJV)* Try something different. Get out there in life. Stop watching TV and living vicariously through the TV characters. Go and live the life of your dreams.

- Be the hero of your own movie. Does life feel shitty, joyless, and hopeless? Do you feel like you are stuck in a rut with no way out? You already know how to get out. Be the hero of your own movie. (This is my favorite.) Pretend you are the hero character in a Hollywood blockbuster. There is a point in every movie where the hero is down and out, with seemingly no way out, yet he always finds a way to overcome the odds. Pretend you are that hero, you are in a tough spot, and it is your job now to overcome the odds and come out on top because it is in the script. Pretend there is a documentary crew following you around, and one day, your kids will see what you have been doing. Do you want them to see a hero who overcomes the odds or a loser who plays the victim? Last time I checked, the hero does not overcome the odds by watching TV for five hours a day. Do what needs to be done no matter how hard it is. March to the beat of your own drum and stay the course. Were you told at any point in your life that your own music was the wrong kind? Re-consider.

Pray always to God and trust in Him. *It is better to trust in the Lord than to put confidence in man.(Psalm 118:8 NKJV)* This is the summary of all the principles of my life, and it should be the bases of yours too. He stands waiting for us to do us good. *For everyone who asks, receives, and he who seeks, finds, and him who knocks, it will be opened.' (Mathew 7:8 NKJV) 'If you then, being evil know how to give good gifts to your children, how much more will your father who is in haven give good things to those who ask him? (Mathew 7:11 NKJV)* I cannot imagine doing anything without God as the center. God's promises are to be fulfilled in us to His glory and honor. Have you ever thought that God's goodness to you when lived out through your life would bring Him glory? *For all the promises of God in Him are Yes, and in Him Amen, to the glory of God through us. (2 Corinthians 1:20 NKJV)* Yes and Amen, so be it, and when we live out loud with His direction and purpose His promises are fulfilled in our lives and He receives glory from a life that reflects His goodness! *For in him we live and move and have our being, as also some of your poets have said, 'for we are also his off springs. (Acts 17:28 NKJV)*

The choice is ours to make. Will we live the life that God has given us out loud with purpose and direction, or will we be carried along by what life brings our way?

Live with intention.
Walk to the edge.
Listen hard.
Practice wellness.
Play with abandon.
Laugh.
Choose with no regret.
Appreciate your friends.
Continue to learn.
Live as if
This is all there is.
—Mary Anne Readmacher

CONCLUSION

Some believe life is pointless, that the purpose of all things would be to be born, then die, and become food for other living things. If Life really had no purpose, why would we be here today? Can we honestly think that our lives were created just to die? There is something we are all meant to do, something that will define our existence, none of us know what it is or how high it is, but it's out there. We are all most likely to do what we were meant to do—fate they call it. The Bible's books are not just written to inspire the goodness in us (like some seem to think). It is a road map, a guide for our life. *Every Scripture is God-breathed (given by His inspiration) and profitable for instruction, for reproof and conviction of sin, for correction of error and discipline in obedience, [and] for training in righteousness (in holy living, in conformity to God's will in thought, purpose, and action), so that the man of God may be complete and proficient, well fitted and thoroughly equipped for every good work.(2 Timothy 3:16-17 AMP)* You cannot throw God out of the picture of your purpose and its fulfillment. He is our maker, he is the one that had put those desires, longings, and thirsts in us, and he alone has the water that will quench it. That is why we thirst and hunger to be known for something that sometimes we cannot explain; we only know that we have a desire seeking to be expressed. We can only fulfill or achieve this quest in us by totally relaying on God and his words. Yes, I know some have 'achieved' without God, but go ask and they will tell you of the emptiness inside still longing to be filled. The search for the purpose of life has puzzled people because we typically begin at the wrong starting point (ourselves). It is God who directs the lives of his creatures; everyone's life is in his power. Life is about letting God use you for his purposes, not you using him for your own purpose.

It is about becoming what God created you to be by focusing on what matters most; God and his words.

My bible tells me, *and he shall be like a tree firmly planted(and tended) by the streams of water, ready to bring forth its fruit in its season; its leaf also shall not fade or wither; and everything he does shall prosper(and come to maturity).(Psalm 1:3 AMP)* When we depend on him, train our focus on him. We are like a tree, whose roots are sunk deep into the earth next to an irrigation stream. Because of this, the tree can flourish even when the going gets tough. This tree drinks deeply from streams of water. Those who depend on God drink daily from God's word. They are resilient, but God watches over the paths they walk. Am I saying that that we should become lazy, do no work, and just depend on God to work it out? No way The Bible clearly has its stand on laziness. ... *If a man will not work, he shall not eat.'(2 Thessalonians 3:10 NKJV)* We put total trust in God and depend on him to have full satisfaction and guarantee of good success. *'Jesus stood and said in a loud voice, "Let anyone who is thirsty come to me and drink."' (John 7:37 NKJV)* Jesus knows that our souls are thirsty— the hunger to fulfill our purpose. Living in our world can be like hiking through the desert. If we do not get enough water, we would not make it. Too many of us are hiking with an empty bottle. We fill it up occasionally or try satisfying our thirst with other things, which only leave us feeling thirstier. *Commit to the Lord whatever you do, and your plans will succeed.' (Proverbs 16:3 NKJV)*

Make a quality decision about your life—a decision that you can never back down at. You stake your life on it. It is easy to get inspired, but to become the winner God wants you to be, it takes more than inspiration. It requires a quality commitment. Do not look for the path of least resistance because if you are prepared to stand forever, it will take very long. You tend to become whatever you give the most attention to.

> ***ONLY THOSE WHO DARE TO FAIL***
> ***GREATLY CAN ACHIEVE GREATLY.***
> *–Robert F. Kennedy*

When you have reached your goal and you are living your dream, be sure to enjoy it. Enjoy the trip, too. Give yourself some rewards along the way; give yourself a huge reward when you get there. Help others enjoy it. Be gracious and generous. Use your dreams to better others then go back and dream a little **bigger** this time!

> *Live with intentions,*
> *Do what matters*
> *And change the world.*
> *–Anonymous*

It can be exciting to be living out a great purpose in life and to know that it is the purpose, which you were born into this world. If you want to find this purpose, may I suggest that you get alone somewhere with God and sort it out with Him. You may find it helpful to pray a prayer something like this:

God, I want to find that purpose for which you created me. I accept that you know who I am, what my gifts are, how my life can count for something meaningful and lasting.

I accept that Jesus died on the cross for my sins because of His great love for me. I thank Him for that.

I am sorry for my sins, I repent of them, and I now accept your forgiveness. Come into my life and begin the process of molding me into all you planned that I should be and directing me in the path you have chosen for me.

Give me the courage and strength to live worthily of your love and to follow this purpose wherever it leads.

Amen.

Impossible is just a big word thrown around by small men, who find it easier to live in the world they have been given than to explore the power they have to change it.
Impossible is not a fact. It is an opinion.
Impossible is not a declaration. It is a dare.
Impossible is potential.
Impossible is temporary.
Impossible is nothing.
JUST DO IT!

Anonymous

REFERENCES

New king James Bible version
Amplified bible version
Mariashriver.com
Qnet.net
National onion association web page
Sermon central
Skills you need.com
Pastor Ose Imiemonhon teachings (The Brook Church, Calabar)
55 motivational quotes-bright drops
Fbcnet.com
Blog.iqmatrix.com
Mind tools.com
Game changer movement.com
www.presbyterian.ca
Mbaskool.com
Becoming a game changer-Andy llapp
http://personalexcellence.co/blog/101-ways-to-live-your-life-to-the-fullest/

    Credit to Celestine Chua

        https:www.facebook.com/onyiiudohbooks
        onyiiudoh@gmail.com
        www.onyiiudoh.com

www.ingramcontent.com/pod-product-compliance
Lightning Source LLC
Chambersburg PA
CBHW071907070526
44583CB00016B/1883